THE STORY OF FOOTBALL

Rob Lloyd Jones

Illustrated by Paddy Mounter

Reading consultant: Alison Kelly,
Roehampton University

Contents

Chapter 1

Ancient ball games

People have always loved kicking balls around. Over 2,000 years ago, the ancient Chinese made balls that were stuffed with goat fur.

They weren't sportsmen, though.
They were soldiers, who booted the
ball into a tiny net hanging high
above them.

Their generals thought it would
improve their aim with weapons.
To get the full battle experience,
just as they lined up their shot...

...the rest of the army charged.

A hundred years later, the Roman army also trained with footballs. Their game involved running with a ball and kicking it over the other team's line. The matches were very fast…

...and furious. Sometimes there were hundreds of players on each side.

7

As the Roman army conquered Europe, they introduced their ball game to new countries — and the very first international matches were played.

Chapter 2

Medieval mobs

Football really took off in Britain. Many people think the Romans introduced it there too, but one story claims it was first played with the head of a Viking prince.

The game quickly became very popular in England – too popular, in fact. When matches were organized between two villages, thousands turned up to play.

The aim of the game was to kick the ball from one village to the other. But matches were really just an excuse for a ferocious fight. While huge crowds gathered to cheer on the players, more nervous spectators stayed safe indoors.

Players chased the ball along narrow streets, over muddy fields and even through bogs and rivers. Games could last a whole day, and sometimes into the next day too.

Throughout the match, players hit each other, bit each other and kicked each other. They even bashed each other with bats. The only thing that wasn't allowed was murder.

The game caused so much damage that, in 1314, the Lord Mayor of London banned it from the city's streets.

But no one listened to him. By then, football had too many fans.

Chapter 3

"We need some rules"

In the 19th century,
smaller teams of boys
began to play football in
schools throughout Britain.
Teachers hoped the game would
teach them strength, courage and
how to work as a team.

Football now moved from the streets to special school playing fields known as pitches. Each pitch had goalmouths at either end for the teams to score. There were still no set rules, though. Each school simply made up their own.

Some allowed players to trip each other up.

Some allowed them to kick each other in the shins.

And others even let them pick the ball up and run with it.

As long as they all used different
rules, no two schools could play each
other. So, in 1863, students from
several schools and universities in
England met to decide exactly how
the game should be played.

Most importantly, they decided that players were not allowed either to handle the ball or trip each other up.

The group named themselves the Football Association (F.A.) and their new sport became known as soccer. Soon, it was being played on parks and pitches across England.

At last, soccer had rules, but it was a very strange game to watch. Players wore thick socks, heavy cotton shirts and even hats.

For extra grip, they screwed sharp studs into the bottom of their boots – and quickly started wearing thick wooden shinpads outside their socks.

Early soccer pitches were unusual
too. Some had ponds in the middle,
which were covered over before each
game. A team from Newcastle had
the oddest pitch of all – it sloped
from one end to
the other.

As teams, now of 11 men, played more games, they began to organize themselves into set positions.

Goalkeepers guarded the goals, where opposition players tried to score.

Defenders defended the goal.

Midfielders usually played in the middle of the pitch.

Wingers stayed out on the sides...

...and **strikers** scored the goals.

23

The first matches played were all friendly games. Then, in 1871, the Football Association created a knock-out tournament named the F.A. Cup. Fifteen teams played in the first competition, which was won by the Wanderers, from London.

The Wanderers were lucky to
reach the final. Their semi-final
opponents only dropped out
because they couldn't afford the
train fare to the match.

25

One of the biggest changes to soccer took place in 1880. The F.A. decided to introduce referees to make sure there was no foul play during matches. Referees had to stand out from the players, so they wore fancy dinner suits.

At first, they simply waved a handkerchief if they spotted a foul.

It wasn't until 1970 that referees were given special cards to punish misbehaving players. A yellow card was a warning...

...and red meant the player was sent off the pitch.

Chapter 4

Going global

As more and more people began to travel abroad in the 19th century, they took soccer balls with them across the world.

Before long, the game was being played everywhere, from Australia to South America.

In 1904, a new group – the International Federation of Football Associations, or F.I.F.A. for short – was created to make sure every country played by the same rules.

As soccer spread around the globe, different players added their own special skills...

...and surprises to the game.

In 1930, a new competition was created between different nations – the World Cup. Thirteen countries entered the first tournament, which was held in South America.

It didn't get off to a great start. In the opening game between Mexico and France, the referee blew the final whistle six minutes early. By the time he realized his mistake, the players were already in the baths.

He made them pull their muddy kits back on and finish the game.

Even so, the first World Cup was a huge success. Over 100,000 fans packed into the stadium to watch the final between Uruguay and Argentina on July 30, 1930. Uruguay won the game 4-2.

The competition grew into one of the biggest sporting events in the world. In 1934, 32 teams played. By 2010, 205 nations entered, but only the top 32 qualified for the finals in South Africa.

Every year, soccer gets bigger and bigger. Today, there are over one and a half million teams across the globe. Some play in huge grounds, which can seat up to 100,000 fans.

Teams are grouped together in leagues, and every year they play each other to decide who's the best. Players in the richest leagues can be paid tens of millions of pounds and are as famous as movie stars.

Not all leagues are so well off.
The Isles of Scilly, off the coast of
Britain, only has two teams in its
league and they play each other
every single week.

Chapter 5
Rugby rules

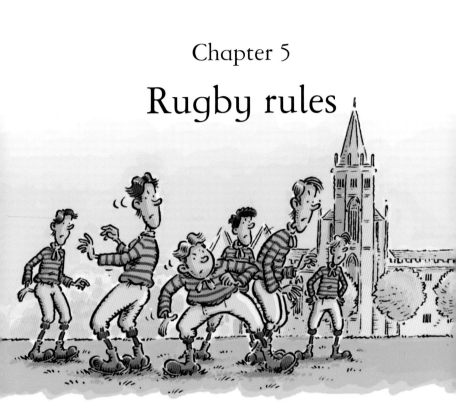

Despite its popularity, not everyone wanted to play soccer. One story claims that, during a match in 1823, a student named William Webb Ellis decided he'd rather carry the ball than kick it.

His teammates were confused, but the crowd went crazy.

Soon, other schools were playing this new game too. They named it Rugby Football, after William Webb Ellis's school, and used oval-shaped balls that were easier to handle and throw.

The main rule of rugby was that players couldn't pass the ball forward. But it was just as chaotic as early soccer, with hundreds of players fighting for the ball. Everyone loved these pile-ups, which they called scrummages.

And there was one part of the game that they loved even more...

...the rugby tackle.

In 1895, a new form of rugby
was created called rugby league. It
had fewer players and pile-ups, but
became just as popular.

Rugby found fans all over the world, first in Europe, then Australia, New Zealand and South Africa.

During the First World War, a match was even played beside the Egyptian pyramids.

In Ireland, the rules of rugby mixed with soccer to create a game that was similar to both, known as Gaelic (say Gay-lik) Football.

A similar game to rugby is also played in Australia, known as **Australian Rules Football**. Players score goals by booting the ball between towering posts.

But when rugby reached
America, it changed into
something completely different...

Chapter 6

American Football

Footballs have been kicked about America for over four hundred years. As early as the 16th century, Native Americans played a game known as *pasuckuakohowog*.

Teams of up to 1,000 people tried to kick a ball between posts that were 800m (half a mile) apart. It was pretty rough stuff. The players even wore disguises in case they killed one of the opposition.

Then, at the end of the 19th century, rugby arrived in America. Games were organized between different colleges and schools.

At one college, a man named Walter Camp felt the game could be made even better.

So he changed the size of the pitch, reduced the number of players in each team, and allowed players to pass the ball forward.

American Football was born.

Like soccer and rugby, American Football was originally a violent, brutal game. Players used tactics such as the flying wedge, in which they linked arms...

...and hurled themselves at the opposition.

Sometimes the player with the ball crawled along the ground for protection, or was dragged to the goal line by his teammates.

American Football players began to hide padding in their shirts to shield themselves against the bone-crunching tackles.

But it didn't help. The sport was so rough that, in some games, players even died. Eventually, it was decided that American Football players needed protective clothing – a *lot* of protective clothing.

Getting kitted out

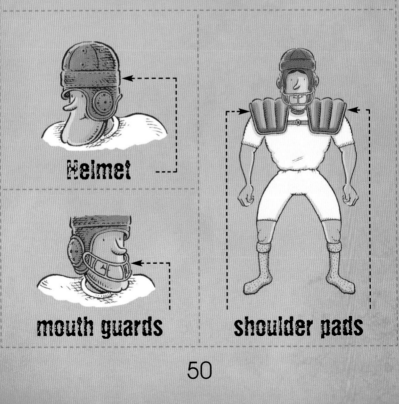

Helmet

mouth guards

shoulder pads

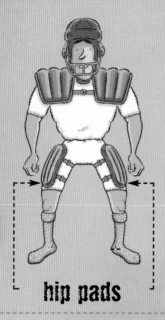

hip pads

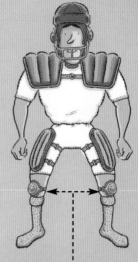

knee pads

shin pads

toe caps

By the 1950s, television
broadcast American Football
games across the nation. More and
more people began to support their
local teams and the players
became huge stars.

Today, over 150 million people around the world tune in to watch the biggest game of the year, known as the Superbowl.

Chapter 7

Strange matches

Football matches have been played
in the strangest places and times —
even during the First World War.

On Christmas Day in 1914, British and German soldiers played soccer against each other. When the games ended, they returned to their trenches and the war went on.

Almost thirty years later, during the Second World War, a team from the Ukraine named Dynamo Kiev were forced to play a game against an enemy German side. The Germans had given the team a grim warning...

56

But the players refused to be bullied – they were playing for their national pride. So they pulled on their boots, ran out onto the pitch and won the game 5-1.

After the match, several of the players were arrested by German army officers and killed.

One of the strangest soccer games ever took place in 1945, when Arsenal played Dynamo Moscow in London. As the game began, there was so much fog that players couldn't even see the ball.

Both teams decided to use the bad weather to their advantage. When an Arsenal player was sent off, he crept back on again. Then the Russian side sneaked four extra players onto the pitch.

As the fog grew thicker, things turned even more chaotic. The Arsenal goalkeeper ran into a goal post and knocked himself out – and was then replaced by a member of the crowd.

Today, football matches still arouse incredible passion. Over 240 million people play in teams around the world – that's 1 in every 25 people on the planet. So wherever you are, you're never far from someone kicking a ball.

Football facts and dates

200BC - Ancient Chinese soldiers kick footballs to improve their aim.

100BC - The Roman army begins booting balls too.

13th century - Vicious villagers play fierce football in English streets.

Early 19th century - Football finds fans in English schools.

*In the **19th century**, footballs were made from pig bladders, which were blown up like balloons. Often, they were so smelly that no one wanted to go near them.*

1823 - Players pick up the ball... and Rugby is born.

1863 - The Football Association is formed, and fouling is banned.

The name 'soccer' comes from the SOC in Football AsSOCiation.

New types of football develop all over the world, including Australian Rules (**1858**), American Football (**1874**), and Gaelic Football in Ireland (**1887**).

*Goal nets were introduced to soccer pitches in **1891**, so players could tell if they had scored or not.*

1930 - The first soccer World Cup kicks off in South America. The cup itself is known as the Jules Rimet trophy, after the man who created the competition.

*Football players began wearing numbers on their shirts in **1933** so referees would know who they were.*

*The World Cup itself was stolen in March **1966**. One week later, it was found in a bush by a dog named Pickles.*

1967 - The first American Football Superbowl is played to decide the top team in the USA.

*Perhaps the foulest football game ever took place in **1975**, between Chile and Uruguay. Of the 22 players who started the game, all but three were sent off.*

1987 - The first rugby World Cup is played in Australia and New Zealand.

2010 - 205 countries enter the 19th soccer World Cup, in South Africa. The final is watched by over a billion fans around the world.

Football consultant: Dr. Tony Collins, International Centre for Sports History & Culture, De Montfort University

Series editor: Lesley Sims

Designed by Neil Francis

First published in 2007 by Usborne Publishing Ltd., Usborne House, 83-85 Saffron Hill, London EC1N 8RT, England. www.usborne.com
Copyright © 2007 Usborne Publishing Ltd.

64